THINK

FROM FEAR TO FAITH

Madeline Soto

Copyright © 2023 Madeline Soto
All rights reserved
First Edition

PAGE PUBLISHING
Conneaut Lake, PA

First originally published by Page Publishing 2023

ISBN 979-8-88960-011-4 (pbk)
ISBN 979-8-88960-019-0 (digital)

Printed in the United States of America

For God have not given us the spirit of fear,
but of power of love and a sound mind.

—2 Timothy 1:7 KJV

DEDICATIONS

First, I give honor to my Heavenly Father
and my Lord and Savior, Jesus Christ,
who gave me this vision to write.

To my father and mother, who showered me with
love and determination to be the best that I could be.

To my loving husband, who struggled
along with me through this process.

To my daughter, who inspires me, and to my
brother, who never stops encouraging me.

To all who read this book and are blessed by how
God still uses ordinary people like me to speak
faith instead of fear into the hearts of his people.

THE SLIDING BOARD

My first and only granddaughter Monet was delightful and full of energy as most little girls are at four years old. Monet was visiting with us for the weekend in our apartment in the northeast section of Philadelphia. She arrived that Friday night after attending preschool that morning. I thought that she would be tired from having a full day, not her. I myself had worked all day and was very tired. Saturday morning, of course, she woke up early and was ready to go.

"What are we doing today?" she asked. I told her that we would go to the playground later that afternoon. To Monet, afternoon was in a minute. The time was 9:00 a.m. The playground was only right across the street from the apartment. Off we went to our first outing of the day. She was always excited to go outdoors. When we arrived, she started on the merry-go-round and then the seesaw where she left me on to the swings. I thought after a while she would ask to go on the sliding board but to my surprise, she refused to get on it. I asked her why she wouldn't get on the sliding board and her answer was, "I'm afraid." I asked her why she was afraid, and she said her mother and other grandmother don't go on anything that is high. So we began to talk about her fear of heights. I remember us having this conversation a while ago with her, but here is a teachable moment. I taught her many scripture verses one such verse, "For God has not given us the spirit of fear, but of power of love and a sound mind" (2 Timothy 1:7 KJV). When I started reciting the verse, she finished it and realized that she could repeat what she learned. Now was the time to put words into action. I walked to the sliding board beside her, and as she went up the stairs, I told her if she started to become afraid, ask Jesus to go with her to protect her. The first time she said, "Come on, Jesus," and sled down the sliding board I was in front for her to see me as she landed. Then she ran around and proceeded to go again saying, "Come on, Jesus."

The third time going up the stairs, Monet said, "I don't want Jesus to go with me." After being afraid to get on the slide board, Monet's attitude changed from I'm afraid to I don't need help, I got this. Does that sound familiar? Once we are sure that we feel safe that is when we feel like I don't need you now, I got this. I told Monet that she did not have to say "Come on, Jesus" out loud as she was doing; she could say "Come on, Jesus" in her mind.

And then she whispers, "Come on, Jesus."

Children are sponges, and they listen to what adults say and watch what they do. We are the teachers, and we teach what we know. Do we want them to grow up fearful? I hope not. Now, I'm teaching that same lesson to my great grans. "Train up a child in the way he should go, and when he is old, he will not depart from it" (Proverbs 22:6 KJV). This is a warning to parents not to let a child continue in a life filled with fear of people, places, or things; instead, teach them to have faith. The word of God needs to be more than words, they are to be put into action.

The lesson that was taught on that day applies to every area of our lives and is not just for children that have a fear of sliding on a sliding board. That story happened twenty-five years ago. Now Monet has three children of her own, and I pray that the lessons she was taught are being passed down to them to have faith, which is the opposite of fear. I teach what I believe, and faith works for me (Deuteronomy 6:7 ESV). Teach them diligently to your children, talk to them when you are at home, and when you are walking along the way, when lying down, and when you wake up. If you talk the talk, you should walk the walk. Don't be a hypocrite. This is one of several stories told in this book concerning how children deal with the matter of faith. Jesus said, "Let the little children come to me, and do not hinder them, for the kingdom of heaven belongs to such as these" (Matthew 19:14 KJV). Children are pure in heart and not polluted with cares of the world. In the next story, you see how faith can continue to work in the lives of children that I have encountered over the years.

THE STORM

Jameen is who I called my praise child. My second granddaughter had health problems at birth, but she has been a blessing to me. My daughter called me up to share this story with me. There was a rainstorm on that concise day. Michelle told me that it was thunder and lightning at that time. Jameen had bowed legs, and her mom said that she noticed that she would be running into things, so she started wearing glasses at a very early age. On this rainy day, Jameen heard thunder and began running through the rooms, quoting scripture (2 Timothy 1:7 KJV). I can only imagine seeing her running, repeating God has not given me (and still running) the spirit of fear (running seeing lightning) going as fast as her little legs could carry her, still saying (but of power, love, and a sound mind) finally reaching her mother's loving arms safe from the storm. Here the scripture is in action from a little child. Only in her mind that the word of God works. She was not with her parents when she was running away from the storm. Her mother said that you should have the expression on her face as she was running. Michelle said that it was priceless. Most children and even some adults are frightened of storms for one reason or another. Storms are a part of life; no one has ever said that we would be exempt from them. When they come, and rest assured that they will come. How will you handle it? With fear or faith? The choice is yours. Jameen chose faith which is the word of God. She wasn't crying, running through the house she was reciting what she was taught and believed. God has given us another way to fight the good fight of faith. "Out of the mouths of children you have ordained perfect praise" (Psalm 8:2 KJV). There would be less stress in the world if there were more people that have faith. If you have tried everything else, why not give faith a try? This book is written for adults to see how simple life can be by watching the example of these children. They have inspired me (children) to step out on faith to complete this book.

THE LAUNDROMAT

(Matthew 25:35–40)

This story happened many years ago. I considered myself at that time to be a night owl because I worked at an overnight job—shopped at night. That was then, and this is now. One night or around the wee early morning hours, I went to the laundromat located on Chelten Avenue in Philly. My little Chevy Chevette was full of clothes that I was going to clean.

As I was getting in my car, my son walked up to the car and said, "Where are you going? Can I go?" He hopped in the car and away we went to the laundromat. When we arrived, there was a woman lying on the bench sleeping and two children there. My son had purchased a slice of pizza and gave it to the little boy who said that he was hungry. My clothes were in the washers and dryers. I asked the little boy why he and his sister were in the laundromat. He said he was with his mother. I asked the attendant if he knew the children, and he said that he let them stay there overnight because they were homeless. As my clothes were finishing, I bagged up my clothes and proceeded to the door and I turned around and the mother of the children woke up.

I asked her if I could help her, and she replied, "I need a place to live." You should never ask a person if I can help you if you do not want to help. That is what I heard when the Holy Spirit spoke to me. He asked me, "What are you going to do?" What do you think I did? I crammed them in my little car and brought them to my brother's house, a duplex. I must tell you that it was a remarkably busy morning. My son helped with the little boy's care. My daughter helped with the little girl, I helped the mother. I let them sleep overnight.

The next morning, which was a Sunday morning, I called my pastor and said that I needed clothes for them. It was wintertime, so I went to the store and brought gloves and hats for the children. I also brought food and prepared breakfast. I took them to church with me, and we met with my pastor and a social worker that was a member of our church. My pastor talked with the mother of the children and told her that we wanted to help her to go to treatment for her addiction and find a place for her children. The woman first said that she had no one to care for her kids. She told me about her sister and we called the sister and the social worker, and I transported the children to their aunt. Praise the Lord, it was a good outcome. Faith is the reason for this story because when I see people suffering, I put myself in their place. I have a daughter and son, and I said that could have been me. Most people question why I do the things I do, and my response is not I but Christ that dwell in me. I said it before I am a faith walker, I do what the Lord says (Malachi 3:10 ESV) test me, and see, prove me. The Lord loves what he says and so do I. I thank God for my family and church for love.

> For I was hungry, and you gave Me food; I was thirsty, and you gave Me drink; I was a stranger, and you took me in; I was naked, and you clothed Me; I was sick and visited Me; I was in prison, and you came to Me. "Then the righteous will answer Him, saying, Lord, when did we see You hungry and feed You, or thirsty and give you drink? When did I see You a stranger and take You in, or naked and clothe You? And the King will answer and say to them, Assuredly, I say to you, inasmuch as you did it to one of the least of these My brethren, you did it to Me. (Matthew 25:35–40)

THE RASH

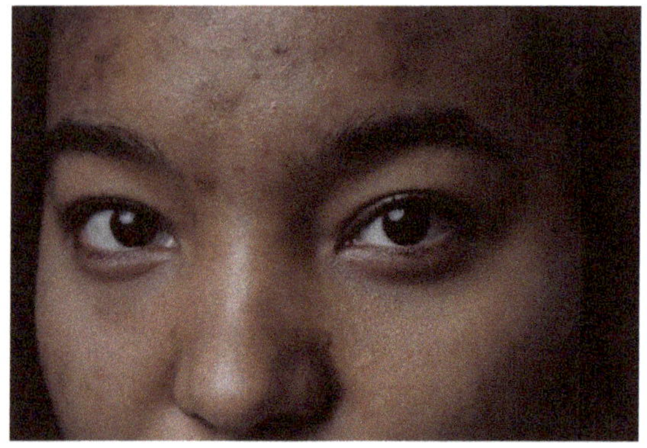

Without faith it is impossible to please him, for whoever would draw near to God must believe that he exists and that he rewards those who seek him.

—Hebrews 11:6 KJV

Skin rashes can have causes that aren't due to underlying disease. Examples include hot and humid weather, excess sun exposure, or scratchy clothes that don't fit.

Monet, my granddaughter, has always been a constant presence in my life. Every weekend, she is growing up before my eyes. She's my son's only child.

On this one day, Monet visited, and when she arrived, she told me, "I started not to come over and stay with you today."

We worked on one of my jobs. One of my part-time jobs is working for American Greetings displaying cards in stores, so we worked late that night and rose early that morning to go to church. I noticed that there was a rash on Monet's face. We talked about the rash for a moment. We kept it moving. At some point during the day, I said let's pray about this rash.

I laid my hands on her face and said, "Thank you, Lord, for Monet. Thank you for her life. Now in the mighty name of Jesus, we praise you in advance for healing Monet this rash. You must go in Jesus's name." We prayed together and believed the rash to go. Both Monet and I saw later that the rash was gone.

Later, Monet said, "I know if I came to your house, you would pray for me. That's why I came. I heard it said, prayer is the key, and faith unlocks the door." The rash that Monet had was a mustard seed compared to healing diabetes, cancer, etc. God is waiting to heal you whatever the problem. Believe, receive, it's yours. Don't be a faith talker, be a faith walker. If you have 'ever experienced the power of God, you would believe and have faith. Thank you, Lord, for using me to share these stories with your people—the ones that know you, and the ones yet to come.

THE ROAD TRIP

The Family That Prays Together, Stays Together

The year was 1999, and a few family members were on their way to High Springs, Florida, for a family reunion. My brother, Jake, drove his son, Benny; his daughter, Angie; and my oldest granddaughter Monet, and of course, yours truly. You know if you travel with young people, you must keep them entertained, at least back then. A few years ago, we had a tragedy in our family that was still fresh in our minds. Moving right along, we were coming from Philadelphia, Pennsylvania, and we had a long drive ahead. Stopping for gas, the rest stop and food. The children were ages as young as eight and as old as ten. My brother drove all the way there and back not because I did not offer to help with the driving. In the beginning was excitement, then drama, and restlessness; sixteen hours of longing for arrival to our destination. The question on everyone's mind— are we there yet? How many families do you know that agree? The family I grew up in had five children. There was always tension between us and then the parents—seven in all, four males, three females.

Now the drama begins. We stopped to get something to eat. We went into the restaurant and Angie said, "okay, let's order something to eat." Everyone picked from the menu selection, and we waited for the food. Monet was sitting next to her uncle, Angie's dad, and Angie said Monet was trying to take her dad from her. While waiting, Jake asked Angie why Monet was trying to take her dad. She said just because she is. The food had arrived, and we began to eat. We tabled the discussion until we got in the car.

Monet said to Angie, "I share my dad with you, and I did not get upset."

Angie was still not happy with Monet and replied to her statement and said, "Again, you are still trying to take my dad."

Angie's dad said, "How do you think we should settle this problem?"

Angie responded, "Let's go to the Jerry Springer Show."

I laughed, but it was only funny to me because she thought that was a good solution to the problem. Angie's dad said how could Jerry Springer help.

She replied, "We could fight it out." How many people think like my niece? That's the best way to solve their problems? My brother was puzzled. I shared that when Angie came home from school with her grandmother and watched the Jerry Springer Show daily. Angie said, if her grandmother approves, it's ok. Children watch adults and do what they see them do. There was another issue. Angie was being raised by her dad, and her mom was not in the picture, so she felt that she only has him. My brother said that he never thought about anything like that. All children need to feel safe and concerned about someone taking the only person that they feel secure with. She needed reassurance from her dad that no one could come between them. Love wins all problems. My niece taught my brother and myself that she is telling how she feels, but we must listen. When I spoke about tragedy earlier, it was the loss of Monet's dad. Maybe that is why Angie feels the way she does, and even Monet clings to her uncle. Praise the Lord, we arrived safely in Florida. Angie and Monet were playing like usual, all was well. Helping each other keeps the family in praying for one another and together. Love is the answer, not Jerry Springer Show.

CIGARETTES

I was a cosmetologist for thirty years, and on some occasions, I went to customers' homes. On this day, I was also taking care of my granddaughter. Her mom was working and I was the sitter for that day. Jameen was watching a cartoon, and the client was sitting with hair color in her waiting for it to process;

so she took the cigarette out to smoke it, and Jameen said the angels are sad.

My client said why are the angels sad, and she said, "You are getting ready to smoke that cigarette." Now, as you read in another story, she is my praise baby. My client put the cigarette out, and Jameen said, "Yeah, the angels are smiling now because you put the cigarette out." My client said, "I'll never smoke around her again." Both my client and I were amazed how she responded to the cigarette. Jameen was three years of age but concerned about my client smoking that cigarette. Children are very sensitive to spiritual things. I believe that angels are real. One thing for sure she got both our attention. My client said that she would never smoke around her again, and she never did. Perfect praise. Did Jameen hear that smoking was hazardous to health? Who knows. Did my client stop smoking cigarettes? No, she did not smoke around Jameen. Why am I talking about this story? Children observe far more than we think they do they need to be pointed in the right direction. My son asked me one time why do people smoke if they know it is bad for them. I told him people make choices that are good for them and bad for them. You suffer the consequences of bad choices. Jameen taught a good lesson; you must be mindful of what you do around children, and when they speak, listen. They might teach you something.

*****

No name cigarettes
A lesson from my son

One Sunday, my children and I were sitting in an afternoon service. The minister was expounding on the scripture, and he mentioned no name cigarettes. How God see everything we do—we fool people, but we can't hide from God. My son was sitting right behind me, and he said he was talking about you. I was guilty. I couldn't get upset because he was telling the truth. I was just talking about being mindful of what you do around children. This a story that happened when my son was young before Jameen was born. Doing wrong always comes to you to remind that you'll reap what you sow. The Lord delivers me from no name cigarettes. When I thought about writing the story of cigarettes, this came to mind about the no name cigarettes.

THE CITIZEN ARREST

Love your neighbor as thyself.
—Leviticus 19:18 KJV

I believe that when someone is in need of help, God uses ordinary people. I believe when the Holy Spirit places something in your mind to do, and you don't obey—you are in disobedience to the Holy Spirit of God. I was on my way home from Bible study one day, and my daughter was with me.

I had worked earlier that day then we went to Bible study that evening. Our church was in Mount Airy, Philly, and I lived in the northeast, and I was tired. I was on route 95 and I was ten minutes away from my apartment and one truck was driving in and out all the lanes and no one would pass him. Well, I'm a fool for Christ sake. I speeded up to the pickup truck and told the driver to pull over. I pulled over behind him and asked the guy first if he was all right. I asked him to pull his window down, and we talked for about five minutes. I could tell that he had been drinking. I told him that I was concerned and wanted to know if he would be able to drive home safely. After we talked, he thanked me for stopping him. I asked him if he wanted me to follow behind to make sure he arrived home safely, but he said no. I asked him if I could call him to make sure he got home safe. He gave me his number; I called when I arrived home myself. When I called his wife answer and I told her who I was, and she thanked me and shared that she had already been in trouble for drunken driving, and she thanked again and said that he was home. I shared this story, because you need to be led by the Spirit of God. Do not do what I did. I was concerned not just for him but anyone in his path.No fear—faith alone. I have so many testimonies like this. One, for people to see how God uses ordinary people. I am his child, and if he can use anything, he can use me. My daughter said that she was afraid while I was talking to the man while she waited in our car. I told her how God has used her to be a witness to how God can use us for His good, but we must depend totally on him.

THE ARBITRATION

God judges the righteous.
—Psalm 7:11–12

I have worked in the field of caregiving for twenty-five years. I have worked with children in special need classes, adults with physical disabilities, people with mental illness, and seniors. I love helping people; and recently, retired after fifty-five years in two careers. This story is one that's a first for me because

I never went to an arbitration with a union representative and defended myself. Let us begin.

I was working on a job with a consumer that was bipolar and needed care 24-7. On this day, I have work overnight—11:00 p.m. to 7:00 a.m.— and I got a call from the person that was supposed to relieve me, informing that she was going to be an hour late. I could not leave; that would be an automatic termination for abandonment. In which I work as unto the Lord, so I waited until my relief arrived. She arrived at 8:00 a.m., an hour later. My time sheet reflected that one hour. I was off from work until my next shift a few days later. My job called me to tell me that I was suspended pending the outcome of the investigation. I needed to call the union, and they would tell me the details. The union representative said that I had falsified some documents. I was out of work for two weeks, and I got a letter from the job saying that I was terminated for falsifying my time sheet for one hour of pay. The amount was $12. Why would I lose my job for that amount? I had to become an investigator. I prayed and asked the Lord for direction. "Seek first the kingdom of God" (Matthew 6:33 KJV). I had to backtrack and find the person that relieved me. When she arrived on-site that night, that was the first time I worked with her. I had to confirm with her that one difference, and when I talked to her, she documented her time an hour from mine. The union representative informed me of the date set for the arbitration. The Lord had already let me know that I was vindicated. I even prayed about what to wear, can you believe it.

I was on my way to arbitration and thanking the Lord as I go. I met the union representative at the office meeting room. We talked for a while before the hearing started. I had a notebook and pen and so I came to take notation of what was said. The CEO of the company started the meeting and heard someone say after a thorough investigation that I was being terminated for falsifying documentation.

Now, it was my turn to speak and ask them a question, "Are you sure that you thoroughly investigated this matter?" And they replied yes. I asked them again who they said relieved me that day, and they told the coworker's name. I told them that she didn't. I also told them the name of the person that relieved me that day. We took a break, and after that, the company said we will recess and return in five minutes.

The union representative said, "You prove them wrong, and they are not going to be happy with you after this." The company started the section again and found that there was an error on their part, and they apologized with loss wages paid right away. The company asked me if I wanted to start work that night, and I said no. They asked me if I had anything to say, and I told them that I wanted an apology in writing. Vindicated. The Lord fought my battle, and he is the righteous judge. He did it for me, he can do it for you. "For the Lord God is a sun and shield: the Lord will give grace and glory: no good thing will he withhold from them that walk uprightly" (Psalm 84:11 KJV). The union asked me If I wanted to be a union rep., and I turned it down. I try my best to be humble like a child, and that way, God can use me. Doing the right thing always pays off in the end.

BEING ALONE

Be strong and of good courage, fear not, nor
be afraid of them: for the Lord thy God, he
it is that doth go with thee; neither forsake
thee: fear not, neither be dismayed.
—Deuteronomy 31:6

My one and only daughter Michelle, when she was born, I thought they gave me the wrong baby. She looked like an Eskimo. She was my living doll, and when she was little, she said, "Do you think that I am a doll baby?" She was the first child, and I fussed over her. I always wanted a little girl. She didn't stay small for long. As a matter of fact, she grew up too fast. Michelle hated me fixing her hair because I would pick with it all the time. The next thing you know, she's in high school. Her brother, Bookie would not let any of his friends talk to her. He was very protective of all the girls and woman in the family. Bookie was our very own bodyguard. Well, now Michelle had a boyfriend, and his name was Stanley. He was a nice young man—well-liked. He was about three years older than she was, and the family attended the same church. He lived in the neighborhood. I know his parents and his siblings. Whenever Stan came over to visit, everyone would be around.

One day, Michelle said to me, "Stan and I never get a chance to be alone." *Alone.* That word echoed in my mind. I realized where this was going. Oh, no. I had to do something but what? It was almost like someone had given me some bad news. It was hard for me to wrap my head around the word *alone.* My baby girl was really a teenager, reality has set in. I wish her dad had been around for this time. It was all on me, so I would not let this day go by without dealing with the word alone.

I told Michelle we were going to be alone today. We went to lunch, shopping until late that night. I had alone on my mind. I thought about being celibate, a word I never heard before. I remember having a virgin pin that was worn by most of my friends. It was popular in my generation. I told Michelle I wish I had never been alone with her father. I had not been alone with her father although I thank God every day for my daughter and son. I got married right out of high school, too young.

My Michelle went to college, got married at twenty-one, and had her first child five years later. She is now an author and grandmother, praise the Lord. To God be the glory. This is me an adult-child leading my children, but I thank God for my mom, father, and family. My parents would not allow us to be fearful. They had faith.

THE MOVE

Now the Lord had said unto A'bram, get thee
out of thy country, and thy kindred and from thy
father's house unto a land that I will shew thee.
—Genesis 12:1 KJV

After being in Philadelphia for seventy years of my life and the home that my husband and I had lived in for over twenty years, we moved. We sold the house, packed up, and relocated. It was more than a notion. We decided to move a year or two before the actual event. Now, I woke up a few years before with Florida on my mind. I asked the Lord why I was thinking of Florida. I asked the Lord, "What do you want me to do?" Go to the land which your forefathers had for you. It is not just for you it is for all the family, but you go first and get things started. The land has been vacant for over forty years, and your father wanted you to be on that land. Was this move easy? Not at all. I see it differently. My life has never been about me; it has been about the family. Faith is how we have got this far, not fear. Since we arrived in Florida five months ago, we have been from hotel to apartment. Talking about the apartment, we were looking for apartments in Jacksonville, Florida. I was having a problem with my cell phone, and my husband suggested that we look for another one. We went to Cricket to see what they had, and my husband was not satisfied with the selection, so he went to T-Mobile while I stayed in Cricket. I told the young man about moving from Philly to Florida and told him that we were looking for an apartment. He said that his grandmom had a one-bedroom apartment. He called his grandmom, and without any red tape, we went to meet her and see the apartment. We filled out an application, and we gave her a few days so she could check the references, and she called in a few days. We moved in two days. I thank God for that young man every day for calling his grandmom. God gave us favor, and I'm looking forward to getting to the promised land, and my eyes are on the prize. I have support from family and friends who care and know me. God has made it less stressful than it would have been without him. Obstacles? No problem, the Lord has given us a way of escape. The story continues. It is unfolding as I write. I'm a faith walker and continue to press forward and I am waiting for my change to come. It's coming.

THE HEALING

But He was wounded for our transgressions,
He was bruised for our iniquities; The
chastisement of our peace was upon Him,
and by His stripes, we are healed.
—Isaiah 53:5 NKJV

When I turned sixty years of age, I was diagnosed with diabetes and hypertension. I said to myself what was going on with my body. It must be breaking down. I was taking medication for both problems. I need to mention that I do not like taking medication. At one point, I asked the doctor if my blood sugar levels are not a concern Why do I need to continue taking medicine? My blood pressure was good also. What was the point besides pharmaceutical companies making money and doctor's getting a benefit from the medicine companies? Now, I took the prescription for years. My husband and I found out about a supplement that helps with high blood pressure and diabetes and many other medical concerns, so I started taking the supplements that are infused in the coffee tea and capsule forms. My husband and I became distributors of the product. I told you that I'm a faith walker and I stopped taking prescription and just took the supplement. It has been six years now, and every time I go to doctors to get blood work and get my pressure taken, no problems to report. By faith, I believe that I am healed.

One doctor said, "Whatever you are doing, it is working. Keep doing it." The same physician told me, "You are one of the healthiest people in my clinic. Again, I do not recommend that you stop taking your medications. You have your own measure of faith." Is there anything too hard for God? Not in my book. I can't begin to tell all that I've seen him do. This is the Lord's doing, and it is marvelous in our sight. Jesus is my healer, my life, my everything. He is the way, the truth, and the life. I brought a pendant many years that says "Try God" one way the Lord has allowed me to witness. I forgot I have it around my neck on a chain. People comment on it every time they read it. I pray that my great-grandchildren will read this book, and they will know my heart—not only them but anyone who reads it. I hope this is a help. I remember talking to an aunt years ago when we talked about divine healing, she said that she did not believe in it. I did then, and I do now. It is by your faith that you are healed. Read the word of God for yourself. You must believe that he is, and he is a rewarder of them that diligently seek him. He said, "Test Me put Me to the proof and see won't I what I said." He is patiently waiting, that is what he does. You must choose who you will serve—the God of faith or the god of fear.

MONEY

If you lack the means to pay, your very
bed will be snatched from under you.

—Proverbs 22:27 NIV

Today, we are all concerned, and the prices are continuing to rise. I was taught by my mother that if you do not handle money, it will handle you. When I started working, it seemed to me that I could not hold on to a dime. I would even spend money that I did not have. Am I the only person on earth like this? I used to teach Bible study at a women's prison for seven years, and I would ask the inmates if this scripture was true "Money is the root of all evil," and most would say that it was true. For the love of money is a root of all kinds of evil. Some had strayed from the faith in their greediness" (1 Timothy 6:10 KJV). Jim Jones started off which I believe on the right track, but money and lust distorted his way. In 1973, The O'Jays sang a song "For the Love of Money."

> Some people got have it, some
> people really need it,
> do bad things with it, people still
> from their mother brother,
> will lie, cheat, don't care who they
> hurt or beat women
> sell her precious body don't let
> money fool you.
> They call it lean, mean, mean
> green.
> Money is just money it does not
> have feeling people do.

Have you ever been guilty of any of the things described in the song above? "I used to buy things and could not pay my bills." One time, I worked three jobs for things. I would borrow money and avoid people that I owed. Ten years ago, I started praying and asked the Lord to help me handle money. I needed a car, I asked the Lord for help. He is a very present help in the time of trouble. I had a car, but the mechanic that worked on it said that I would not put any more money into this car. I did not have any money for a car, my credit score was low. I went to two dealerships, and they said that they could not help me. My husband said that I'm not going to get a car. I told him that is not what the Lord told me. I got two nos, and I refused to give up until I got a yes. The third try at the car dealer, I walked in, told him I needed favor, and said I have no money. I didn't have good credit.

The dealer said, "You sure do." I said that I lived in Philly, and I worked down the street in Warrington where the dealership was. I owed $2,500 for the car I had. I sold it, and I got paid that week and needed $1,800 down. My husband cosign for the loan the dealer came to my house for my husband to fill out application. Guess what, he was a minister. The car was brought to my job and I told the dealer, don't cash the check until Monday. The dealer wanted me to trade my old car in, and I told him that I was giving the car to my granddaughter who was in college at the time. I made my first car payment on time. The finance company sent me a letter saying that they could not finance the car. The dealer said, "You did have the favor of God." I have purchased several cars since then with the help of the Lord. The Lord is still helping with financing money and everything else. He said, "In all your ways, acknowledge him, and he will direct your path." I am retired now, and I had one income of my own—a fixed income—but he keeps me. I used love. When my grands where young and they wanted something, they would ask their parents, they would say to they don't have the money to do whatever, they said "call mom-mom." People that know me, call me for money and asked why do you think I have money, and they say you always have money. I tell them that the Lord is show- ing me that I must be mindful of when to spend and when to save. One of my grandchildren was in the car with me because I was taking her home, and we were passing a McDonald's and she asked me if she could get something from there and I said that I didn't have any money. She replied you have a mac card. I told her that a mac is no good if you do not have money in the bank. I am trying to help the next generation with how to invest their money, savings, etc. I wish

I had been around people that had knowledge of keeping money. Now, I know the difference between needs and wants. The Lord supplies my needs and the Lord is my shepherd and I shall not want. As you get more seasoned in life, you learn to know the difference between buying just to buy. I don't require much these days. There are many more stories of how God helps in handling money. Do not let the cares of this world keep you in bondage or money be your Lord. "A fool and his money are soon parted" (Proverbs 21:20). Take heed of good advice. If you can't stand for something, you will fall for anything. We definitely have to have money in this world, but you don't have to be a slave to it. Money is a tool to be used.

THE BICYCLE

Therefore, we do not lose heart.
—2 Corinthians 4:16 NKJV

Though outwardly we are wasting away, yet inwardly we are being renewed day by day. Recently, I purchased a bicycle. I remember when I was young, I enjoyed biking—the wind in your hair, you decided where you wanted to travel and how far and what direction to choose. It was fun as well as keeping me fit. I am over sixty now and really wanted to see if I could still do it without breaking my neck. They say once you learn how to ride a bike, you never forget. They never told you as you get older, you must be able to lift your legs up high enough to get on the thing. It is more than a notion; it is work, but when you realize you can, it is a plus. The first bike I purchased was red, one of my favorite colors. There were a few glitches. It was a mountain bike, and I could not get my leg over the bar. It was supposed to be a unisex bike. I was fooling myself thinking that I could be comfortable maneuvering that bike. I refused to waste away. After all, I retired three years ago, I needed to exercise this young body, and I have been coloring in adult books for the last five years. Riding the bike gave me more flexibility. I like controlling my own time. I needed to renew the way I managed my time. My body is being renewed day by day, but I need to take care of my temple. The first bike did not work for me, so I needed to return it and get one that worked for me. I had to remind myself of my age and that I had not ridden a bike for at least twenty years or more. A Huffy twenty-six-inch Cranbrook Women's Comfort Cruiser bike, that was more my speed. The first run on the bike was a half an hour fifteen minutes there and back, it felt good. The last time I rode, it was an hour, and I felt like the bike was giving me energy. I told everyone I knew about my bicycle. I was excited about the bike, but of course, like all new things, you lose interest. I mentioned earlier that I love coloring adult coloring books because not only does it relax me, but it also helps me think. When I attended elementary school, my favorite thing was to do anything artistic. I write this story to encourage the old and young of all ages to enjoy your life to its fullest. Don't fear death, fear the unlived life. I tell my grandchildren that I am a mover and a shaker—that's me. I'm a young older person. To God be the glory for what he has done in my life. When my mother was alive, I showed her a picture of herself, and she said who was that old lady. My sister and I had brought an outfit for her on Mother's Day, and I asked my husband to take a picture of that outfit on. Mom had a stroke, and it affected her short-term memory. That is why she did not recognize herself sometimes and forgot my name. I remember my mom said that she used to ride a motorcycle. That was cool. I would not mind trying that next. What you do with your life that makes you happy is what counts. Just like Nike says,

"Just do it," life is short. Depending on what you do with is what counts the most. No fear but faith. If no one believes in you, believe in yourself. I thought that this book was just about other children and how they deal with fear and faith, but I realized that I am one of the children the Lord told me to write about. This is how I see life now that I am a Christian and have been for over forty years. In the writing of these stories, I see how God has changed my way of seeing from a different perspective.

THE BIRTHDAY PARTY

(1 Corinthians 13:11 ESV)

When I was a child, I spoke as a child, I understood
as a child, I thought as a child; but when I
became a man, I put away childish things.

Monet is four years old now, and today she's
having a birthday party. The party was being
held at her grandparents' home in Mount Airy in

Philly. She was the only first grand of both dad and mom. My husband's cousin had a business providing children characters, clowns that do face painting, and entertained the children with games. That was our present to Monet. At that time, Monet loved Barney's television show, so Barney arrived at her party. And when I arrived, she was sitting on her grandfather's lap. I asked Monet why she was in the basement and Barney was upstairs. Her grandfather said that she feared Barney. Now, Barney is over six feet purple and furry dinosaur so to a four years old little girl, I might be frightened too. Monet and I talked about fear as we have many times before. Remember God has not. She said, "I know given me. The spirit of fear but power, love, and a sound mine." She got off her granddad's lap and went upstairs. I talked to her granddad for a while then I went upstairs. Children were all over the house on every corner and saw Monet standing next to Barney, and she said, "I was afraid of you, but I'm no more." I asked Monet if she was having a good time, and she said yes. She also said that she was afraid of Barney but not anymore. I told her that Barney was at her party as per her request. The parents all agreed that they enjoyed the party because Barney and the clowns entertained the children so that they could socialize with the other parents. Children adapt so much easier than adults. All they need is encouragement and so do adults.

Monet's grandfather said, "I'm glad you talked to her."

The theme of the story teaching faith supersedes and replaces fear. Try it, and see that it works. Faith walkers know what I'm talking about. After all, faith is an action word. Put your faith to work; if it's not working, give it a job.

ABOUT THE AUTHOR

Madeline Soto was born and raised in Philadelphia, Pennsylvania. She worked as a cosmetologist and a caregiver for fifty-five years. She was also a licensed minister of the Gospel of Jesus Christ and was passionate about soul-winning. She enjoys singing, writing lyrics to songs, and coloring in adult coloring books. She is happily married to Mike, whom she calls her knight in shining armor. She has two children, four grandchildren, and five great-grandchildren.

www.ingramcontent.com/pod-product-compliance
Lightning Source LLC
Chambersburg PA
CBHW040112150726
48005CB00013B/1669